PIANO • VOCAL • GUITAR

COLE PORTER
Love Songs

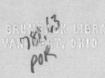

ISBN 0-7935-8956-8

HAL•LEONARD®
CORPORATION

7777 W. BLUEMOUND RD. P.O. BOX 13819 MILWAUKEE, WI 53213

Visit Hal Leonard Online at
www.halleonard.com

Broadway Melody of 1940 (Film).
Eleanor Powell and Fred Astaire
dance to a Cole Porter tune.

COLE PORTER
Love Songs

CONTENTS

COLE PORTER
A Brief Biography

by Elaine Schmidt

Cole Porter, c. 1950s.

The witty, urbane songs of Cole Porter made their first appearance on Broadway (1916) a full decade before the New York public was ready for them. Not until Rodgers and Hart and the Gershwin brothers had broken away from the silly comedies of the teens and popularized an image of urban-chic was the Broadway stage ready for Porter's catchy rhythms and flippant, clever rhymes. Once that ground - work was laid, Porter's music and his wildly clever lyrics came to define the decade of the 1930s. While most composers found success in sob-ballads and syrupy love songs, Porter was at his best in his settings of society verse and his signature "list songs," such as "You're the Top." Yet his brilliantly inventive, seemingly endless catalogs of comparatives and superlatives, which left audiences breathless and amazed, meant little to him. He most aspired to write straight-faced, sincere love songs.

Clad in exquisitely tailored suits, an ever-present flower on his lapel, Porter's enormous personal family fortune, polished manners and position in high society circles made him an anomaly in Broadway circles. Born to a wealthy Indiana family in 1891, Porter was educated at Yale and Harvard. He was groomed from early on to take over the family business interests in his native state. Thanks to his mother, an accomplished amateur pianist, he received musical training from an early age. It was her intervention that eventually freed him from his grandfather's demands that he study law and take over the family business. At Yale, Porter's charm, social skills and ability to invent comic songs won him the friendship and respect of his peers. Spending far more time at the piano than at his studies, he led the glee club and worked on musical and theatrical productions. The football songs Porter wrote as a student are still heard on campus today.

Porter entered the Harvard Law School in 1913. He hated his law studies from the outset. When his grandfather finally relented, Porter quickly shifted over to the Harvard School of Music. Porter's music took a leap from witty, risqué party-songs for the college set to the Broadway stage in 1916. Still a student at Harvard, he saw his first show, *See America First*, panned by critics as "the newest and worst musical in town." They accused Porter of copying Gilbert and Sullivan and George M. Cohan in that single show. (How could that be possible?). The doomed production closed after a run of less than two weeks.

In 1919 Porter sailed for France where he became the darling of Parisian socialites and American expatriates, including the wealthy, American, divorcée Linda Lee Thomas. He and Thomas married in 1919, beginning a stormy relationship that would continue until her death in 1954. With Europe as their playground, the Porters kept lavish homes. They frequently threw extravagant parties that featured Cole holding court at the piano entertaining his guests with his music. In these years Porter provided songs for a New York show entitled *Hitchy-Koo of 1919* and a 1925 Yale Dramatic Society production. Eventually a Paris nightclub revue he wrote brought an invitation to write the score for the New York production *Paris* (1928), which featured the songwriter's first famous song, "Let's Do It." The winning blend of sophistication, off-hand wit, naughtiness, and common-man vernacular that would become his trademark finally charmed Broadway.

While the 1929 stock market crash left the Porters' fortunes largely unscathed, most of their society friends were not so lucky. The party of the Roaring Twenties had ended. The Porters returned to New York, where Porter quickly became the toast of Broadway, and pushing the censorship of the day to its limits with his double entendre. During the 1930s Porter wrote more than one hundred songs for Broadway, and ventured into Hollywood with three film scores. From 1928 to 1937 was Porter's heyday. His musicals on Broadway included:

Fifty Million Frenchmen (1929)
    featuring the song "You Do Something to Me"

The New Yorkers (1930)
    featuring the naughty/fun/obliquely poignant
    "Love for Sale"

Gay Divorce (1932)
> starring Fred Astaire singing "Night and Day"

Anything Goes (1934)
> his most successful show of this period, including "I Get a Kick Out of You," "You're the Top," and the title tune, and introducing Ethel Merman to Broadway

Jubilee (1935)
> including "Begin the Beguine" and "Just One of Those Things"

Red, Hot and Blue! (1936)
> again starring Ethel Merman, featuring "It's De-Lovely" and "Down in the Depths (On the Ninetieth Floor)"

Then tragedy struck in 1937. Porter was riding a horse on a friend's Long Island estate when the horse fell, crushing both of the composer's legs. Complicated by a chronic bone infection, the accident damaged his nervous system, required more than thirty operations over the next twenty years, and left him in constant pain. Deeply depressed following the accident, Porter followed his doctor's advice and threw himself back into his work, creating *Leave It to Me* (1938). The show was the auspicious Broadway debut of Mary Martin, with her signature number "My Heart Belongs to Daddy." Porter continued his relationship with Broadway star Ethel Merman in the 1939 musical *DuBarry Was a Lady*, which included the naughty "But in the Morning, No" and the sarcastic "Well, Did You Evah?" *Panama Hattie* opened in 1940, with Ethel Merman as star, and although none of the songs have survived as standards, the show was Porter's longest running to that time, with a run of 501 performances (an unusually long run for the period). *Let's Face It* (1941) had a longer run of 547 performances. *Mexican Hayride* opened in 1944, and although successful, it continued a disturbing trend in Porter's work: the lack of hit songs. That had been largely true of his scores since 1938. Had the master lost his touch? Or was it the changing musical and theater scene?

Believe it or not, Cole Porter virtually disappeared in the mid-1940s for a couple of years. Broadway had changed enormously in the wake of *Oklahoma!* and the supremacy of the book-musical, which was a very different aesthetic from the lightly-plotted musicals of the 1930s. In one of Broadway's greatest comebacks he scored a great artistic and commercial triumph in the 1948 musical *Kiss Me, Kate*, which featured a story-within-a-story adapted from *The Taming of the Shrew*. The show combines Porter's cleverness and wit with characterization and sincerity. In one number, "So in Love," Porter somehow

combined wit, style satire and sentimentality. That song and a few others ("Another Op'nin', Another Show," "Too Darn Hot," "Always True to You in My Fashion") put Cole Porter back on the A-list of hit songwriters. The show charmed audiences throughout the world, playing in translation in cities from Berlin to Rio de Janeiro to Tokyo. It had the unlikely distinction of being the American musical performed in Poland.

The success of *Kiss Me, Kate* (1,070 performances) revitalized Porter's career on Broadway. *Out of This World* (1950), *Can-Can* (1953) and *Silk Stockings* (1955), several hit songs and several films (including the 1957 Gene Kelly musical *Les Girls*) followed, but Porter's health and energy were failing. The amputation of his right leg in 1958 sent him into a downward emotional and physical spiral. He stopped writing music, sank in despondency and withdrew into virtual seclusion. He died in 1964. In all, Cole Porter had composed 23 Broadway musicals in his lifetime.

While Cole Porter's "list songs" have yet to be matched in style or cleverness by another composer, he longed to write the sort of sentimental love songs so popular on Broadway and Tin Pan Alley. When he did set his hand to love songs, at times the often-edgy tone of his lyrics reflected both a level of ambivalence about romance along with a naughtiness that tested the bounds of propriety and acceptability. The combination gave them a bittersweet taste of reality.

Since his death, Cole Porter's songs have lived on as pop and jazz standards. They have appeared in jazz renditions by countless artists, arrangements performed by symphony orchestras, and even on albums of rock performers. The universal appeal of Porter's music and lyrics is attested to by the diverse collection of artists whom have taken turns at recording his songs. Recordings of "Night and Day" have been made by Johnny Mathis, The Beatles, Charlie Parker, Lawrence Welk, U2, Billie Holiday, Chicago, and Dionne Warwick, to name a few. "I Get a Kick Out of You" can be heard in renditions by Ethel Merman, Ella Fitzgerald, the Royal Philharmonic Orchestra, Mel Torme, The Jungle Brothers and Carol Burnett with Julie Andrews, among dozens of others. "In the Still of the Night," from the film version of *Rosalie* (1937), was recorded by jazz pianist Oscar Peterson, cellist Yo-Yo Ma, the Neville Brothers, Rosemary Clooney, The Four Freshmen, Nelson Eddy, The Platters and a long list of others.

Red, Hot and Blue! (1936, Broadway).
Ethel Merman and Bob Hope.

Silk Stockings (1957, Film).
Cyd Charisse and Fred Astaire.

Jubilee (1935, Broadway).
Mary Boland and Melville Cooper.

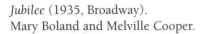

Les Girls (1957, Film).
Mitzi Gaynor, Kay Kendall, Gene Kelly, Taina Elg.

Leave It to Me! (1938, Broadway).
Mary Martin.

At Long Last Love

from YOU NEVER KNOW

Words and Music by
COLE PORTER

All of You
from SILK STOCKINGS

Words and Music by
COLE PORTER

Fox Trot Tempo

With bounce, not too fast

After watch-ing her ap-peal from ev-'ry an - gle,

There's a big ro-man-tic deal I've got to wan - gle.

For I've fall-en for a

All Through the Night

from ANYTHING GOES

Words and Music by
COLE PORTER

Begin the Beguine
from JUBILEE

Words and Music by
COLE PORTER

Between You and Me

Words and Music by
COLE PORTER

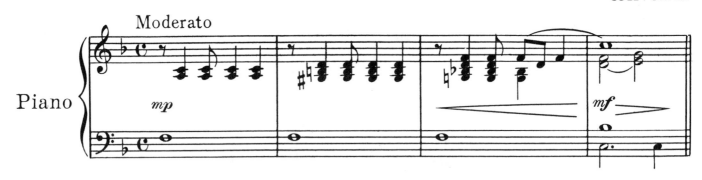

As you sail your glo-ri-ous way Like a shin-ing star,

You don't know what hav-oc you play And how up-set-ting you are, For so

near you seem, At night when I dream, But when I wak-en, How far!

Refrain (*slowly and with warmth*)

Be-tween you and me, You're some-thing spec-

tac-u-lar,— Be-tween you and me, You're a

prize.— Be-tween you and

Ca, C'est L'amour
from LES GIRLS

Words and Music by
COLE PORTER

*pronounce: sah, say

Could It Be You

Words and Music by
COLE PORTER

A white sea-shore in moon-light im-mersed, A si-lent palm-tree sway-ing,

When out of no-where you sud-den-ly burst, And I found my-self say-ing:

Do I Love You
from DUBARRY WAS A LADY

Words and Music by
COLE PORTER

Easy to Love
(You'd Be So Easy to Love)
from BORN TO DANCE

Words and Music by
COLE PORTER

I know too well that I'm ____ just wast-ing pre-cious time in

think-ing such a thing could be, That you ____ could ev-er care for me,

I'm sure you hate to hear___ That I a-dore you, dear, But grant me, just the same, ___ I'm not en-tire-ly to blame, For

Refrain *(slowly, with much expression)*

You'd be so eas-y to love, So eas-y to i-dol-ize, all oth-ers a-bove, So worth the yearn-ing for, ___

Ev'ry Time We Say Goodbye

from SEVEN LIVELY ARTS

Words and Music by
COLE PORTER

Ev'rything I Love

Words and Music by
COLE PORTER

From Alpha to Omega

from YOU NEVER KNOW

Words and Music by
COLE PORTER

From Now On
from LEAVE IT TO ME

Words and Music by
COLE PORTER

From This Moment On
from OUT OF THIS WORLD

Words and Music by
COLE PORTER

I Am in Love
from CAN-CAN

Words and Music by
COLE PORTER

I had no flare for flam-ing de - sire,

But since the gods gave me you to a - dore,

I may lose, but I re - fuse to fight the fire!

So, come and en - light-en my days and nev-er de-part.

I Concentrate on You
from BROADWAY MELODY OF 1940

Words and Music by
COLE PORTER

I Am Loved
from OUT OF THIS WORLD

Words and Music by
COLE PORTER

Moderato (*Slow Fox-trot tempo*)

Yes - ter - day _____ was a dull day, _____

Yes - ter - day _____ was a gray day, _____ But

I Get a Kick out of You

from ANYTHING GOES

Words and Music by
COLE PORTER

I Happen to Be in Love

Words and Music by
COLE PORTER

Keep it qui-et, keep it dark,— But last ev-'ning in the park,—

Par-don me if I re-mark,— I met— my doom.

I Hate You, Darling

from LET'S FACE IT

Words and Music by
COLE PORTER

I Love Paris
from CAN-CAN

Words and Music by
COLE PORTER

more ... do I re - al - ize

Slow Fox Trot

I love Par - is in the spring - time, _____

I love Par - is in the fall, _____

I love Par - is in the win - ter, when it driz - zles,

I Love You
from MEXICAN HAYRIDE

Words and Music by
COLE PORTER

I've Got My Eyes on You

from BROADWAY MELODY OF 1940

Words and Music by
COLE PORTER

I've Got You Under My Skin
from BORN TO DANCE

Words and Music by
COLE PORTER

In the Still of the Night
from ROSALIE

Words and Music by
COLE PORTER

Let's Do It
(Let's Fall in Love)

Words and Music by
COLE PORTER

It's De-Lovely

from RED, HOT AND BLUE!

Words and Music by
COLE PORTER

I feel a sud - den urge to sing,— The kind of dit - ty that in-

vokes the Spring, So con - trol your de - sire to curse while I cru - ci - fy the

Pronounced "delukes".

IT'S DE-LOVELY

VERSE 2

She: Oh, charming sir, the way you sing
  Would break the heart of Missus Crosby's Bing,
  For the tone of your tra la la
  Has that certain je ne sais quoi.
He: Oh, thank thee kindly, winsome wench,
  But 'stead of falling into Berlitz French
  Just warble to me, please,
  This beautiful strain in plain Brooklynese.
She: Mi, mi, mi, mi,
  Re, re, re, re,
  Do, sol, mi, do, la, si
He: Take it away.

REFRAIN 2

Time marches on and soon it's plain
You've won my heart and I've lost my brain,
It's delightful, it's delicious, it's de-lovely.
Life seems so sweet that we decide
It's in the bag to get unified,
It's delightful, it's delicious, it's de-lovely.
See the crowd in that church,
See the proud parson plopped on his perch,
Get the sweet beat of that organ, sealing
 our doom,
"Here goes the groom, boom!"
How they cheer and how they smile
As we go galloping down that aisle.
"It's divine, dear, it's diveen, dear,
It's de-wunderbar, it's de victory,
It's de vallop, it's de vinner, it's de voiks,
 it's de-lovely."

REFRAIN 3

The knot is tied and so we take
A few hours off to eat wedding cake,
It's delightful, it's delicious, it's de-lovely.
It feels so fine to be a bride,
And how's the groom? Why, he's slightly fried,
It's delightful, it's delicious, it's de-lovely.
To the pop of champagne,
Off we hop in our plush little plane
Till a bright light through the darkness
 cozily calls
"Niag'ra Falls."

All's well, my love, our day's complete,
And what a beautiful bridal suite,
"It's a d-reamy, it's de-rowsy,
It's de-reverie, it's de-rhapsody,
It's de-regal, it's de-royal, it's de-Ritz,
 it's de-lovely."

REFRAIN 4

We settle down as man and wife
To solve the riddle called "married life,"
It's delightful, it's delicious, it's de-lovely.
We're on the crest, we have no cares,
We're just a couple of honey bears,
It's delightful, it's delicious, it's de-lovely.
All's as right as can be
Till, one night, at my window I see
An absurd bird with a bundle hung on his nose—
"Get baby clo'es."
Those eyes of yours are filled with joy
When Nurse appears and cries, "It's a boy,"
"He's appalling, he's appealing,
He's a polywog, he's a paragon,
He's a Pop-eye, he's a panic, he's a pip,
 he's de-lovely."

REFRAIN 5

Our boy grows up, he's six feet, three,
He's so good looking, he looks like me,
It's delightful, it's delicious, it's de-lovely.
He's such a hit, this son of ours,
That all the dowagers send him flowers,
It's delightful, it's delicious, it's de-lovely.
So sublime is his press
That in time, L. B. Mayer, no less,
Makes a night flight to New York and tells him he should
Go Hollywood.
Good God!, today, he gets such pay
That Elaine Barrie's his fiancé,
"It's delightful, it's delicious,
"It's delectable, it's delirious,
"It's dilemma, it's delimit, it's deluxe, it's de-lovely."

Mind If I Make Love to You

Words and Music by
COLE PORTER

Night and Day

from GAY DIVORCE

Words and Music by
COLE PORTER

Ours

Words and Music by
COLE PORTER

Refrain *With great feeling, but in a steady flowing rhythm*

Ours, _____ the white_ Ri - vi - er - a, un - der the moon,_

Ours,_____ a gon - do - la

glid - ing on a la - goon,_ Ours,_____ a

tem - ple ser - ene by the green Ar - a - bian Sea, or

Paris Loves Lovers
from SILK STOCKINGS

Words and Music by
COLE PORTER

So in Love
from KISS ME, KATE

Words and Music by
COLE PORTER

know, dar - ling, why, _____ So in

love _____ with you am I, _____ In

love with the night mys - te - ri - ous, _____ The

night when you first were there, _____ In

love   with   you,   my   love_____   am

True Love
from HIGH SOCIETY

Words and Music by
COLE PORTER

Moderately Slow

mf

poco rit.

a tempo

G **C** **Gdim** **G**

I give to you and you give to me

D7 **C** **G**

True Love, True Love. So, on and

C **Gdim** **G** **D7**

on it will al - ways be True

What Is This Thing Called Love?

Words and Music by
COLE PORTER

You're Just Too, Too

from LES GIRLS

Words and Music by
COLE PORTER

You Do Something to Me

from CAN-CAN

Words and Music by
COLE PORTER

And I gazed at you. Won't you tell me, dear, Why, when you ap - pear, Some-thing hap-pens to me And the strang - est feel - ing goes through me?

Slowly, with expression

Refrain

You do some-thing to me.

You'd Be So Nice to Come Home To

from SOMETHING TO SHOUT ABOUT

Words and Music by
COLE PORTER

Allegretto comodo

Piano

It's not that you're fair - er, Than a lot of girls just as pleas - in', That I

doff my hat as a wor-ship-per at your shrine, — It's

You're Sensational

Words and Music by
COLE PORTER

You're the Top
from ANYTHING GOES

Words and Music by
COLE PORTER